A Taste
of Maple

History and Recipes

MICHELINE MONGRAIN-DONTIGNY

Quebec Cooking Collection

From the same author:
- L'Érable, son histoire, sa cuisine
- La Cuisine traditionnelle des Cantons-de-l'Est
- Eastern Townships Traditional Cooking
- La Cuisine Traditionnelle de Charlevoix
- La Cuisine Traditionnelle de la Mauricie
- Traditional Quebec Cooking
- Délices Traditionnels du Québec
- Saveurs et Parfums des 4 coins du monde: Soupes
- Saveurs et Parfums des 4 coins du monde: Cuisine Cajun et Créole
- 150 Recettes pour le Saguenay-Lac-Saint-Jean
- La Cuisine Rapide
- Légèrement Vôtre

National Library of Canada cataloguing in publication

Mongrain-Dontigny, Micheline, 1950-

    A taste of maple : history and recipes

    (Quebec cooking collection)
    Translation of: L'érable : son histoire, sa cuisine.
    Includes bibliographical references and index.

    ISBN 2-9804058-9-2

    1. Cookery (Maple sugar and syrup). 2. Sugar maple. I. Title.
II. Series: Mongrain-Dontigny, Micheline, 1950-   . Quebec cooking collection.

TX767.M3M6613 2003 641.6'364   C2003-941998-3

Cover design by Sébastien Dontigny
Interior design by Daniel Dontigny
Photographs by Pascale Dontigny, Sébastien Dontigny, Chiali Tsai, Micheline Mongrain-Dontigny

Les Editions La Bonne Recette
www3.sympatico.ca/edition.bonnerecette/
Printed in Canada

to **Pascale**,

for her enthusiasm in searching harmony of taste

to **Sébastien**,

for his creativity and tenacity

Acknowledgements

I would like to express my sincere thanks to my friend and food professional Michelle Gélinas who patiently proofread the recipes of this book.

Table of contents

Introduction

It was my grandfather Antonio Gaudet who introduced me to the mysteries and sweet pleasures of maple. We lived in the second apartment of his house and, every spring, he would tap the two maple trees that stood on his yard for the single purpose of teaching the syrupmaking process to his grandchildren. When we visited him around mealtime, he would offer us enormous pieces of taffy that we gobbled up willingly.

Because of those sweet memories, and like every food lover in Quebec or elsewhere, I am bewitched by that unique taste that flavours desserts, meats, fish and seafood, vegetables and salads.

Who were the first to make maple products, the Amerindians or the French? What varieties of maple are tapped for their sap? You will find answers to these questions as you go through this book. You will also learn the history, ancient and modern collecting and making methods as well as tips for the creation of your own maple-tasting meals. Because of folklore tradition, the Quebec people speak of "sweet water" meaning "sap". Because the exact word is sap, it is used in all the texts, except for a few quotes in historic texts.

This collection of recipes includes modern dishes as well as the essential traditional delights of our grandmothers. I invite you to prepare the following meals and to enjoy the tastes that flavour them: maple-flavoured mussels, beef with beer flavoured with maple and savory, baked beans with maple syrup, dumplings in maple syrup and fruits in maple cream sauce!

The world
of maple

Source: Canada Science & Technology Museum

History

Transformation of maple sap is part of the heritage that was passed on by the North American Indians to the Europeans that came to settle in the New World. In order to extract sap from the maples, the Amerindians made a tap hole in the trunk and inserted woodchips that directed the sap to a recipient made of birch bark. Then, they would pour the precious liquid in earthenware containers to which they added burning stones to cook the sap until it became sugar. The cool stones were constantly replaced with burning stones, until it was properly cooked.

Some wonder if it was whether the Amerindians or French settlers who were the first to transform maple sap; food historians have documented proof that the Amerindians were the first to make maple products. They taught their techniques to the first French settlers that came to North America. A few texts, among which the account of a French named Thévet written in 1557-58, confirm that sweet sap is an American beverage discovered by the French. Pierre Boucher, a naturalist, was aware of the existence of the sweet water in 1664, because he mentions that it is a liquid "that comes out of the tap hole in the maple". Moreover, in 1688, a companion of Robert Cavelier de La Salle mentions that, when it is boiled, maple sap transforms into "reddish" but delicious sugar. Finally, in 1721, father Charlevoix reports, speaking of the maple sap, that the Amerindians "merely boil it once or twice, to thicken it a little" [TN: in ancient French in the text].

The Amerindians made big quantities of maple products and either used them as flavouring ingredients or food. They traded a large part of the production in exchange for goods necessary to the Amerindian community.

The French settlers were the first white people in America to learn maple tapping from the natives. On the other hand, the latter bettered their sap-boiling techniques by learning to do so in cast iron and copper saucepans brought by French settlers. The first documented evidence of maple sugar making by the settlers dates back to 1691. As early as 1706, Madame de Repentigny states that at least 30,000 pounds of maple sugar is produced every year on the island of Montreal and, in 1728, baron de La Hontan writes that "sugar and syrup are made that strengthen the chest".

FABRICATION DU SUCRE D'ÉRABLE EN CANADA.—D'APRÈS UN CROQUIS DE A. T. BARBEAU

Source: Bibliothèque nationale du Québec

In 1749, Swedish naturalist Pehr Kalm, visiting Montreal in order to list the flora of America, mentions that it was explained to him with details how to make sugar and syrup using sugar and red maples. He learns that large quantities of sugar are sent in France, because it is said to be the best of all sugars for health. Kalm also tells that a mister Chambon gave him a few balls of maple sugar for him to bring back to his country. In the same extract, we can read the following: "When visiting the peasants in the countryside, they give you no other sugar than the maple sugar, that every inhabitant himself gets in the spring". He was also told that "eating too much of that sugar makes you lose your teeth… and it is bad for your health". He learns that the syrup made at the end of the maple season has beneficial properties for the chest and stomach, and it is used to make jams and candied fruits.

The American settlers learned to make maple products from the French, who processed maple sap for a century before transmitting their knowledge to the Americans.

The maple sugar, or "maple molasses", remains for years the principal source of sugar in homes. It is only when sugar made from sugar cane becomes affordable that we see a change in the consumption of maple sugar in Quebec. Only the families that made maple products continued to use it regularly. Maple butter appeared in 1930 and, in 1931, the Canada Gazette published the regulations for classifying maple syrup.

THE TREE

Texts by early explorers and accounts tell us that the maple, the grey betula (yellow birch), the ash and the walnut can be tapped, but it is noted that only the maple sap gives syrup with an exquisite taste. The habit of boiling the sap of trees other than the maple is still practiced nowadays, mostly by Amerindian populations that live in northern regions. A few years ago, Amerindian women from the upper St. Maurice confirmed to me that their families tap birches in order to make syrup.

Sugar maple
(Acer saccarhum)

Sugar maples come from the acer saccaropharum species, which is divided into four: the sugar maple (acer saccarhum), the red maple (acer rubrum), the silver maple (acer saccharinum) and the black maple (acer saccharum nigrum). The best tree to make sugar products is the sugar maple, because its sap contains more sugar than the other maples. Attempts were made to transform maple sap out of North America, but the results were mediocre; people realized it is very difficult to raise the ideal maples in climates other than those of Eastern Canada and North-Eastern United States. Moreover, the spring climatic conditions unique to this part of the continent provoke repeated freezes and thaws that are essential for the sap uptake.

Red maple
(Acer rubrum)

The synthesis of sugar by the tree leaves and its storing into the trunk take place in summer. It is also said that the more leaves a tree has at the same size, the more sap it will produce. It is possible to tap a maple when its trunk has reached a minimum diameter of 8 in (20 cm).

COLLECTING THE MAPLE SAP

The Amerindians using a tomahawk made the first tap holes. A spout sculpted in cedar was inserted in the trunk of the tree and sap was collected in recipients made of birch bark.

L'ÉRABLIÈRE

Source: Bibliothèque nationale du Québec

The arrival of European settlers marked an evolution in the maple sap-collecting techniques. The tomahawk and axe were replaced by the bit brace, the wooden spouts by spiles and birch bark recipients by cedar jugs, ancestors of metal buckets.

La récolte de l'eau d'érable.

Source: Bibliothèque nationale du Québec

The syrup makers start collecting the sap at the first thaws, in February or March. Cold nights during which the temperatures fall below the freezing point followed by daytime temperatures above it please syrup makers.

Before modern methods were invented, collecting sap was an exhausting chore; it takes more than 40 gallons of sap to get a gallon of syrup! Members of the family come, put on their snowshoes and visit every maple, take the bucket full of sap to the barrel placed on a sleigh going to the sap house. These comings and goings are repeated until the barrel is full and ready to be dragged by a horse to the house. In his excellent book, "Le Sucre du pays" [Sugar of the country], ethnologist Jean-Claude Dupont reports that before getting help from cattle and horses, men transported sweet water in yokes strapped on their shoulders, a task carried out early in the morning when the "crust" of snow was still firm.

Some traditional sugarhouses still collect manually but nowadays, tubings, snowmobiles and tractors greatly facilitate the chore. Commercial sugarhouses even acquire compressors to accelerate the flow of the sap to the boilers.

Syrup-making

At the time of the early colony, the settler, accompanied by his "able" sons, goes to the camp situated near the sugar bush. They install poles above a wood fire and hang the big pot used to boil the sap that becomes a sugar mass that they shape into sugar blocks. The sugar is an economical good that ensures provisions in sugar for the whole year. If the run was good, gifts will be offered to the priest, lover and family. Two men can make 200 pounds of sugar in a season; some is kept for the family and the rest is sold at the market or exchanged for merchandises.

The first boils were made in large cast iron cauldrons that will first be replaced by flat steel saucepans before the invention of large evaporators called "Champion", a type of evaporator made by the Dominion & Grimm company. The fire is also frequently replaced with the oil heater or propane gas. Some sugarhouses now use a new inverse osmosis process that allows the extraction of a good part of the water contained in the sap before boiling it. It is a common practice that helps save a lot of energy.

Source: Canada Science & Technology Museum

Boiling consists in evaporating the sap until the desired degree is reached in order to transform it into syrup, taffy or sugar. In average, it takes between 32 and 40 gallons (128 and 160 litres) of sap to get 1 gallon (4 litres) of syrup. In order to avoid overflows during the boiling, a fat skin is hanged above the liquid; if the liquid rises too much, its volume steadies when it reaches the skin. At the end of the boiling process, the syrup is filtrated to get rid of the unwanted particles.

The boiling and handling of sap is an art difficult to master and only the seasoned sugar makers know the secrets for making first-quality syrup, sugar, soft maple sugar and maple butter. The last runs give darker syrup, known as "sap syrup". It is used mainly to cook pastries and candies. People in Valcourt and its vicinity told me they preferred using this syrup to make desserts.

Families among the poorest that didn't own a sugar bush took advantage of the sugaring season by using the lands of governments or lumber companies.

Until about 1918, "foreign" traders, most of who come from Quebec City, Montreal or Sherbrooke, buy most of the sugar makers' production.

They announced their visit on the porch of the church when people came out after the Sunday mass. Later, American buyers who paid twice or thrice as much for the products supplanted "foreign" traders. At the same time, cooperatives were created to collect, transform and sell the makers' syrup. Nowadays, a good number of sugar makers sell their production to those cooperatives, while traditional sugarhouses still sell their products directly to the population.

THE SUGARHOUSE

In order to hide from rain, wind or snow, the sugar makers had the idea of covering the boiling fire with boards or barn doors as a basic roof. It is only in the late 1800s that farmers start to build houses. The sugar bush often is located far from the house, and it is more practical to live in the sugarhouse during the sugaring season.

The season starts at the end of February or in mid-March and ends in April. The running period in each region depends on the geographical and climatic situation of the sugar bushes. Those that are located in the south of the province start and end earlier than those a little further north. By living in the sugarhouse, the sugar maker can chop and stack wood for

Source: Bibliothèque nationale du Québec

the next season and continue boiling late in the evening and even at night when the running is good.

The sugarhouse is divided into two rooms, one for working and one for sleeping and eating. In the working room are rocking chairs, the sugar maker's utensils, the sugar moulds, the taffy paddles, the snowshoes and other working tools. The first sugar moulds were cones made of birch bark attached with a thorn and they were called "pick" [TN: picot or pignoche in French]. Later, moulds sculpted in hard maple, birch or walnut woods take the shape of a heart for the lover, houses, animals, maple leaves, books or liturgical instruments. The heart-shaped mould often bears the initials of the sugar maker and his loved one.

FOLKLORE

It is said the calls of the crows announce the beginning of the sugaring season, while the white butterflies found in the sap buckets signal its end. Apparently, the arrival of the first flight of geese also signals the end of the season.

When the sap is at its best, the sugar maker speaks of "sweet water". To him, "sap" only is a substance that no longer can be used to make syrup.

The sugaring season brings colourful expressions in the mouth of sugar makers. A "sugar fall" is a snowfall during the season and "the sugar fall" is the only important storm of the sugaring season. Pork eaten during the season is a "sugar pig" killed in late fall. A part of the animal is salted and frozen until the next spring. It is time to gather around the sugar maker when the taffy is ready, when it forms a hardened cap on a snowball; the maker pours the hot taffy on the snow and then one has to wait just a minute (!) before dipping his or her paddle and tasting the melting and refreshing treasure.

At the end of the season is storing at the sugarhouse: buckets are cleaned and dried in the sun before being stored until next season.

Source: Canada Science & Technology Museum

THE FOOD

During the 19th century and for part of the 20th, the sugar employed in families that own a sugarhouse come exclusively from maple syrup, taffy and maple sugar. Maple syrup frequently replaces butter on bread. Family and friends got the first meals served at the sugarhouse. Later, the sugar makers began serving meals to everyone who wished to join the sugar and spring fever.

Cooks make traditional ham, smoked at the sugarhouse most of the time, oreilles de Christ, baked beans, eggs cooked in syrup, omelettes, crisp crêpes and boiled potatoes. Dishes are brought and put on long tables full of homemade bread and marinades prepared in the fall. Everyone helps himself/herself and soaks ham, baked beans and pancakes with syrup. At the end of the meal, paddles are distributed and everybody is invited outside to savour taffy on snow... It is the most awaited moment of the sugaring-off party... People keep an eye on the hardening taffy and roll it around the paddle, a moment before it becomes too hard. Then, it is time to go back to the sugarhouse and the party continues, with people dancing and feet stomping to the rhythm of the lively music.

THE PRODUCTS

The resulting products of the first transformations are essentially used to make sugar cakes, a condiment and ingredient for dishes. Some made syrup vinegar even before syrup became popular; a recipe was published in a journal in 1837. To do so, bitter-tasting syrup, obtained from the last run, was used. Syrup vinegar was used in all sorts of pickles. The popularity of syrup rose only around 1890. Afterwards, a large range of products (candies, maple butter, soft sugar) appeared on the market.

These last years, wide ranges of new products were developed for the pleasure of consumers. II is now possible to get jellies, caramels, vinegars, alcoholic liquors, etc....

Maple products now are luxury products, but it was not always that way. Several accounts I have gathered over the last decade confirm that maple sugar was an economic good that replaced brown and white sugar, that were luxury goods at the time. It was only in the 19th century that the price of sugar fell; it was a factor that made the people prefer white and brown sugar, to the detriment of maple products.

The first runs give light syrup with a delicate taste. As the sugaring season goes on, the colour darkens and the taste strengthens. The last runs produce "sap syrup" featuring a strong taste, ideal to make pastries and industrial food products. The traditional observation methods used to measure the boiling of the sap were gradually abandoned and replaced by thermometers, densimeters and colorimeters.

Cooking degree of the sap		
Maple syrup	219°F	104°C
Maple tuffy	238°F	114°C
Soft sugar	238°F	114°C
Hard sugar	243°F	117°C

Note: the given temperatures are guides and they can vary according to atmospheric pressure and altitude.

In order to get a sugar of consistent crystallization, it is stirred until the desired texture is obtained. The sugar is then poured into a mould rinsed with boiling water to avoid adherence to the surface. Traditional moulds are sculpted in the evening or during free times of the sugaring season. Commercial moulds are shaped as squares and give sugar cakes of different weights. The small maple cones were shaped using birch bark cones before the appearance of cones as we know them today.

The province of Quebec produces about 70% of the world's maple products, and most of that production is exported to the United States.

AUTHENTICITY OF THE PRODUCTS

Maple syrup is a pure product, without foreign substances added. Authentic products have a tag saying "pure maple syrup" and they must not bear any inscription that says "maple flavour" and/or "artificial maple essence".

The government implemented a law in 1915 in order to regulate the sale of maple products. Any product imitating maple products could not bear the name "maple". That law was made even more precise in 1930 with the introduction of a classification of syrup into 4 categories. From 1943 on, all retail products had to be classified. Products of the categories "light", "extra light" and "medium" are sold to consumers, while those of categories "amber" and "dark" are used to make pastries, aromatized dairy products, meats, liquors, candies and even some tobacco products.

CLASSIFICATION OF MAPLE SYRUP

The exportation of maple products began in 1915 with a shipment sent to some traders in Europe and soldiers of the First World War. The discovery of the new product created an overwhelming demand. Societies, among which Citadelle is the best known, organized to ensure the product is of perfect quality.

A new quality seal called Siropro was recently implemented for the sale of maple syrup; it guarantees the authenticity and the quality of maple syrup. To obtain that certification, the syrup makers must meet precise standards, follow a formation and have their syrup inspected by an independent organization. The purpose of the initiative is to make sure the products offered to the consumers is of uniform quality.

Canadian Classification		
Canada no. 1	extra light	AA
Canada no. 1	light	A
Canada no. 1	medium	B
Canada no. 2	amber	C
Canada no. 3	dark	D

In 1998, an original step is taken by a group of researchers made of specialists of the Centre Acer and Food Research and Development Centre in order to establish scientific and reliable bases for the characteristics of the different syrups. To do so, Ms. Jacynthe Fortin says a "flavour wheel" was elaborated to allow the evaluation of syrup against stable references, the way it is done for wine, beer and cheese. The characteristics and nuances of syrup can be identified using terms like "golden sugar", "banana", "hay", etc... These steps and the elaborated tools now make up a course available to producers or any other person wishing to explore and learn the mysteries and factors that determine the taste of a syrup coming from a specific soil.

COOKING WITH MAPLE PRODUCTS

The flavour of maple products is unique and bewitching. The biggest challenge when cooking with them is to highlight those precious flavours. Spices or food with a strong taste can easily mask the taste of maple. On the other hand, the use of maple products in disproportionate quantities can overpower the taste of a meal.

Light syrups unveil their subtle scent when tasted with pancakes, waffles, bread and food featuring delicate tastes. Medium and amber syrups, which have a stronger taste, star in cooked meals and pastries.

In order to replace a cup of white sugar with a cup of maple syrup in a pastry recipe, Regan Daley, author of "In the Sweet Kitchen" and winner of two prestigious prizes in cookbook contests, advises to reduce the quantity of liquid in the recipe by 1/4 cup (60 ml). The replacement of cream and butter with synthetic products such as margarine and artificial creams is to be avoided at all costs too.

The cooking of meats and poultries on the grill is to be done over medium heat. The food is brushed with marinade when it is almost completely cooked to prevent darkening.

PRESERVATION

Ideally, maple syrup is bought in small containers. Cans of syrup can be stored for a period of two years at ambient temperature. Syrup can also be frozen, either by putting the syrup in the freezer or in cans.

When you open a can, pour the rest into a container barely large enough; this will prevent the taste of the syrup from being spoiled because of the contact with air.

Maple Products ⇒
1- Vinegar 2- Taffy 3- Syrup 4- Jelly 5- Butter
6- Granulated sugar 7- Sugar loaf

Eggs
and
crêpes

Crisp crêpes

Traditionally, these crêpes are cooked in vegetable shortening or pure lard. Nowadays, as we are aware of the bad effects of saturated fats on our health, they are frequently cooked in vegetable oil. Some like to use water, while others prefer to use milk in this batter; I personally prefer them prepared with milk.

2	eggs	2
1 cup	all purpose flour	250 ml
1/2 tsp	baking powder	2 ml
1/2 tsp	baking soda	2 ml
	A pinch of salt	
3/4 cup	milk	175 ml
	Vegetable oil, for cooking	
	Maple syrup	

1- Beat the eggs with a whisk in a medium-sized mixing bowl until blended and that no trace of egg white remains.

2- In another mixing bowl, blend flour, baking powder, baking soda and salt. Gradually add to beaten eggs. Mixture will be stiff.

3- Slowly whisk in milk and keep stirring until the mixture is smooth.

4- Over medium high heat, heat 1/3 inch (1,5 cm) of vegetable oil in a deep 8-inch (20 cm) cast iron skillet. Pour 1/4 cup (60 ml) of the batter in the skillet and spread with the back of a spoon. Fry until underside is browned when gently lifted. Turn over and fry until browned. Immediately remove from the skillet and absorb the excess oil with paper towels. Keep warm in a 250°F (120°C) preheated oven until ready to serve. Proceed with the remaining batter and serve with maple syrup.

FOOD PROCESSOR METHOD

1- Place the dry ingredients in the food processor's bowl. Pulse to mix ingredients. Beat eggs and milk in a medium mixing bowl. With the motor running, pour in the liquid mixture. Mix until smooth. Once or twice scrape sides of the bowl.

3 to 4 servings

Thin French crêpes

My husband loves these crêpes, especially when I serve them sprinkled with maple sugar and drizzled with pouring cream. This recipe can be used for any type of dish requiring a basic crêpe recipe as well as main course crêpes stuffed with various garnishing. The batter can be prepared 2 to 3 days ahead of time and kept in the refrigerator until it is needed. Before cooking, bring the batter to room temperature and add a little bit of water if it looks too thick.

3 tbsp	butter	45 ml
3	eggs	3
1 1/3 cups	milk	325 ml
1 cup	water	250 ml
1/2 tsp	salt	2 ml
2 cups	all purpose flour	500 ml
1/2 cup	extra water	125 ml
	vegetable oil	

1- Melt the butter over low heat. Mix eggs, milk, water and salt in a blender or with the help of a whisk. Gradually mix in flour and melted butter. Beat until smooth. Refrigerate covered for one to two hours.

2- Whisk the batter and add as much as 1/2 cup (125 ml) of cold water until the batter has the consistency of a thick pouring cream.

3- Prepare the kitchen tools: one 1 ounce (30 ml) ladle, vegetable oil, a large plate and a metal spatula.

4- Preheat an 8-inch (20 cm) skillet until a drop of water jumps on the surface of the skillet. Pour just a little bit of oil and tilt the skillet to cover the bottom. Lift the skillet on one side and pour a ladle of batter; immediately tilt the skillet so that the batter will quickly spread. If necessary remove excess batter.

5- Cook for one minute or until the edges of the crêpe begins to dry; flip over and cook for another 30 seconds until you see a few brown spots when the crêpe is lifted.

PRESERVING CRÊPES

- Crêpes are piled up with a piece of wax paper between each crêpe. Place the pile in a plastic bag and refrigerate for 3 days or freeze for 3 months.

- To reheat, place the crêpes side by side on a cookie sheet and bake a few minutes in a 350°F (180°C) preheated oven.

- To remove crêpes from the pile, take out the package from the freezer 10 minutes before beginning to pull out the desired amount of crêpes.

Large puffy pancake

This dish is an old traditional favourite among Québécois. I love this light and puffy pancake that I would describe as a marriage between a crêpe and an omelette. I usually prepare it on weekend mornings when I want to serve a nourishing breakfast to my family and friends. This dish should be served as soon as it comes out of the oven, as it will begin to deflate a few minutes after it is ready.

8	slices of salt pork	8
3	large eggs	3
1 cup	all purpose flour	250 ml
	A pinch of salt	
1 cup	milk	250 ml
	Maple syrup	

1- Preheat the oven to 400°F (200°C). Place the slices of salt pork in a small saucepan and cover them with cold water. Bring to a boil, remove from heat and immediately rinse under cold running water. Drain well. This will remove excess salt from the salt pork.

2- Whisk the eggs in a medium mixing bowl. Gradually mix in the flour, salt and milk. Set aside. In a large cast iron skillet, saute the slices of salt pork over medium high until lightly browned and crunchy. Remove from the skillet and reserve.

3- Pour the batter in the skillet and bake 20 to 25 minutes until golden brown. Serve with slices of salt pork and drizzle with maple syrup.

2 to 3 servings

French toast

Quebec French toast is a cousin of the "pain perdu" that originates from France. "Pain perdu" is dipped in whisked eggs and Quebec French toasts are soaked in a mixture of eggs, maple syrup and milk.

1	large egg	1
1/4 cup	maple syrup, preferably medium	60 ml
1/4 cup	milk	60 ml
1 tbsp	vegetable oil	15 ml
1 tbsp	butter	15 ml
4	slices of bread	4
	Maple syrup	

1- Beat the egg in a medium mixing bowl. Add the maple syrup and milk and beat until smooth.

2- Heat the oil and butter in a large skillet over medium-high heat. Soak the slices of bread in the egg mixture, let drip to remove excess liquid and cook until golden brown on both sides. Remove from the skillet and place on a paper towel to absorb the excess fat.

3- Serve immediately with maple syrup.

VARIATION

Pain perdu: proceed with the same cooking techniques but substitute the egg mixture by using two beaten eggs to dip the slices of bread.

2 servings

Eggs cooked in syrup

Surprising but true, the eggs are cooked in maple syrup. Many Québécois are familiar with this dish and they find it delicious, but I must admit I was part of the sceptics and I never had the guts to taste it until recently. I must confess: I discovered this is a delicious dish.

2	*eggs*	2
	Maple syrup	

1- Pour just 1 1/2 inches (4 cm) of syrup in a small saucepan.

2- Bring the syrup to a boil over medium heat. Break an egg in a small bowl and gently drop the egg in the boiling maple syrup. Simmer 3 minutes, turn the egg over with a skimmer. To check if the egg is cooked, lift it with a skimmer and gently press the egg white; the egg is ready when the white is firm and the egg yolk soft.

Serve with toasts

Vegetables
and
salads

Oven roasted vegetables

A dish that reveals the natural and unique flavour of each vegetable. It is the type of dish that I bake at the same time as a roast and serve with the main dish. You can substitute one or many kinds of vegetable as long as the quantity is respected.

1 tbsp	vegetable oil	15 ml
2 tbsp	maple syrup	30 ml
1/2 tsp	salt	2 ml
2	carrots, cut in thick sticks	2
1	onion, quartered	1
	Half a small turnip, peeled and cut in thick sticks	
2	beets, peeled and cut in sticks	2
	Freshly ground black pepper	

1- Set the oven rack below center. Preheat the oven to 350°F (180°C).

2- Pour the oil and maple syrup in a medium-sized bowl and add salt. Toss in the vegetables to coat evenly. Spread the vegetables in a single layer on a cookie sheet or a large shallow oven proof dish.

3- Bake 15 minutes, turn the vegetables over and bake another 15 to 30 minutes until the vegetables are tender. Season lightly with pepper and serve.

3 to 4 servings

Candied sweet potato

This dish is the ideal accompaniment for a pork roast. The sweet potato slices are baked in a maple syrup mixture, which gives them a smooth texture.

4	sweet potatoes	4
2 tbsp	butter	30 ml
1/3 cup	maple syrup	75 ml
1/3 cup	cold water	75 ml
	A pinch of salt	

1- Set the oven rack below center. Preheat the oven to 350°F (180°C).

2- Peel the sweet potatoes and slice them 1/2 inch (1,5 cm) thick. Lay the slices of potato preferably in a large cast iron skillet.

3- Add the butter, maple syrup, cold water and salt; cover and bake 15 minutes.

4- Turn potato slices over and bake uncovered for 10 to 20 minutes or until potatoes are tender when pricked with a fork.

4 servings

Maple syrup baked beans

I have learned from Mrs Mélida Cloutier of Sainte-Thècle, in the Mauricie region, that the authentic taste of baked beans can be preserved while reducing considerably the amount of fat originally found in baked beans. To do so, she uses pork rind instead of traditional salt pork.

1 lb	dry white beans	500 g
2	square pieces of pork rind, 4 inches (10 cm) wide with a thin layer of fat of about 1/8 inch (0,5 cm)	2
1	small onion, peeled	1
1/2 cup	maple syrup	125 ml
1 tsp	salt	5 ml
1/2 tsp	pepper	2 ml
	Cold water	

1- Wash the dried beans in cold water and discard damaged beans. Soak beans for 8 hours in plenty of cold water.

2- Drain the soaked beans, rinse well under cold running water and drain again.

3- Place a piece of pork rind in the bottom of an earthenware or a cast iron pot. Cover the pork rind with the beans and bury the onion in the beans.

4- In a small bowl mix the syrup, salt, pepper and a small amount of cold water in a small bowl and pour over the beans. Add just enough cold water to cover the beans. Cover the beans with the other piece of pork rind.

5- Cover the dish and bake about 8 hours at 250°F (120°C) until the beans are tender.

4 to 6 servings

Spinach and goat cheese salad

I was inspired to create this dish when, a few years ago, I tasted a salad flavoured with maple and goat cheese prepared by chef Christian Leveque of Montreal. You will be surprised to see how well these two ingredients blend in a dish. Hazelnuts or pecan nuts are good substitutes to walnuts.

2 cups	*torned spinach leaves, without the stem*	*500 ml*
2 cups	*torned Boston lettuce*	*500 ml*
1/3 cup	*crumbled fresh goat cheese*	*75 ml*
3 tbsp	*chopped walnuts*	*45 ml*
1	*pear, for garnishing*	*1*
	Maple vinegar vinaigrette in sufficient quantity (see index)	

1- Mix the spinach and lettuce in a medium-sized bowl and place on two plates.

2- Scatter the goat cheese and nuts on greens.

3- Halve the pear, core and cut each half in four pieces. Garnish the two plates with the pears.

4- At serving time drizzle the dressing over the salad.

2 servings

Spinach and bean sprouts salad

This nourishing salad can be served without eggs as an accompaniment or with eggs as a light meal.

4 cups	*torned spinach leaves, without the stem*	1 litre
3/4 cup	*bean sprouts, rinsed with cold water and drained*	175 ml
3/4 cup	*grated old cheddar cheese*	175 ml
	Maple syrup vinaigrette (see index)	
4	*bacon slices, cooked and crumbled*	4
2	*hard-cooked eggs quartered (if desired)*	2

1- Put the spinach in a large mixing bowl with the bean sprouts and the cheese.

2- Add the vinaigrette and mix gently. Divide among 4 plates.

3- Garnish with bacon and 2 pieces of eggs if desired.

4 servings

Maple syrup vinaigrette

1/4 cup	vegetable oil	60 ml
3 tbsp	maple syrup	45 ml
1 1/2 tbsp	cider vinegar	22 ml
3/4 tsp	Dijon mustard	3 ml
1/4 tsp	dried thyme	1 ml
1/4 tsp	salt	1 ml
	Freshly ground black pepper	
1/8 tsp	ground Cayenne pepper	0,5 ml

1- Mix all the ingredients and add to the salad when ready to serve. If refrigerated, bring to room temperature before using.

Yield 1/2 cup (125 ml)

CAYENNE PEPPER

Never use your hands when manipulating Cayenne pepper as it can burn eyes and skin. It is recommended to wear gloves.

Maple vinegar vinaigrette

Maple vinegar gives a stronger flavour to vinaigrette. Any maple vinegar can be used in this recipe but I particularly like Cabane du Pic Bois' maple vinegar. This vinegar, made in the Eastern Townships region in Quebec, features a very interesting "woody" aroma.

3 tbsp	*cold pressed sunflower oil*	*45 ml*
2 tbsp	*maple vinegar*	*30 ml*
1 tsp	*chopped fresh parsley*	*5 ml*
	Salt and freshly ground pepper	

1- Mix all the ingredients. If refrigerated, bring to room temperature before adding to the salad.

Meat
and
poultry

Chicken breasts in maple cream sauce

A perfect dish to prepare for a gastronomic meal or a family gathering. Tender chicken breasts coated with a lightly sweetened cream sauce. Serve with boiled rice, green beans or broccoli.

1 tbsp	olive oil	15 ml
1 tbsp	butter	15 ml
4	chicken breast, boned and skinned	4
1	large shallot, chopped	1
1 cup	chicken broth	250 ml
1 cup	white wine	250 ml
1/2 tsp	dried savory	2 ml
1 cup	heavy cream	250 ml
1/3 cup	maple syrup	75 ml
	Salt	
1/8 tsp	Cayenne pepper	0,5 ml
1 tsp	butter	5 ml
1/4 cup	finely chopped red pepper	60 ml

1- Preheat the oven to 275°F (140°C). Heat the oil and butter in a large skillet and sauté the breasts of chicken about 5 minutes on each side or until lightly browned. Put chicken breasts in an ovenproof dish and bake while proceeding with other steps.

2- Add the shallots to the skillet and cook for one minute stirring constantly with a wooden spoon.

3- Deglaze by pouring the chicken broth and white wine in the skillet, add savory and cook uncovered over medium heat until reduced by half.

4- Add the cream, maple syrup and Cayenne pepper. Simmer over medium heat for about 10 minutes until the sauce coats the back of a spoon. Season with salt as needed.

5- Melt the butter in a small skillet and sauté red pepper for one minute, stirring constantly with a wooden spoon. Reserve.

6- Pour a fourth of the sauce on a plate, place one chicken breast on the sauce, garnish with cooked red pepper.

4 servings

Maple chicken with vegetables

This is the type of dish that I like to serve on a cold autumn or winter day. An ideal dish to serve to a family after a weekend outdoor activity.

1	chicken, about 3 lb (1.5 kg)	1
3	cloves garlic, peeled	3
1	medium-sized onion, coarsely chopped	1
1/4 cup	maple syrup, preferably medium	60 ml
1 tsp	dried thyme	5 ml
2 1/4 cups	chicken broth	560 ml
	Salt and pepper	
3	carrots, peeled and coarsely chopped	3
3	celery ribs, cut in large pieces	3
5	sweet potatoes, peeled and cut in four or six pieces, according to the size	5

1- Place the chicken in a large pot and add the garlic, onion, maple syrup, thyme, chicken broth, salt and pepper.

2- Bring to a boil, reduce the heat, cover and simmer over low heat 45 minutes.

3- Add the carrots, celery and sweet potatoes. Cook uncovered 45 minutes, basting the chicken and vegetables every 15 minutes. After 25 minutes, turn the vegetables. Cook another 20 minutes or until vegetables are tender.

4 servings

Grilled maple lamb chops

8	lamb chops, 1 inch (2,5 cm) thick	8
1/2 cup	olive oil	125 ml
2 tbsp	cider vinegar	30 ml
2 tbsp	maple syrup	30 ml
2 tsp	Dijon mustard	10 ml
1/2 tsp	dried savory or rosemary	2 ml

1- Place the chops in a casserole just large enough to fit them.

2- In a small bowl mix the olive oil, cider vinegar, maple syrup, Dijon mustard and savory and pour on chops. Cover and marinate 2 hours in the refrigerator; turn the chops over once while marinating.

3- Preheat the barbecue or oven broiler and grill the chops for a few minutes on each side until medium or medium rare.

4 servings

BARBECUE HINT

Baste food with fat, but do not baste the grill racks. This will eliminate much of the smoke while cooking food as well as the strong smoky taste.

Beef stew with beer and maple

I created this dish for the Canadian Beef Information Center for a campaign promoting Canadian products and flavours. I sometimes cook this dish on my gas barbecue when the weather is hot and I do not want to use my regular oven. See the instructions following this recipe.

2 oz	salt pork, rind removed	60 g
1	instant beef broth cube	1
2 tbsp	boiling water	30 ml
1 tbsp	granulated maple sugar	15 ml
2. tsp	cider vinegar or white wine vinegar	10 ml
1/4 tsp	ground black pepper	1 ml
1 tsp	salt	5 ml
1/2 tsp	dried savory	2 ml
1	(12 oz) bottle amber beer	1
1 1/2 lb	(1 1/2 inches/4 cm) beef stewing cubes	750 g
2	medium-sized onions, chopped	2
2 tbsp	vegetable oil	30 ml

GARNISH

4	potatoes	4
1 tbsp	butter	15 ml
16	medium carrots	16

MARINADE

1- Cut the salt pork in 1/2-inch (1 1/2 cm) cubes and place in a small saucepan. Cover with cold water, bring to a boil, drain and rinse under cold water.

2- For the marinade, dissolve the beef bouillon cube in two tablespoons of boiling water and pour in a large glass or stainless steel mixing bowl. Add the maple sugar, vinegar, pepper, salt, savory and beer. Stir well.

3- Place the beef cubes, onions and salt pork in the marinade, cover and marinate in the refrigerator for 4 to 6 hours.

COOKING

1- Preheat the oven to 375°F (190°C).

2- Remove the beef cubes and onions from the marinade and reserve the marinade.Dry on paper towels. Heat half of the vegetable oil in a large skillet and sauté the meat. Remove the cubes from the skillet and place in a 2 quarts (2 litre) casserole or equivalent. Sauté the remaining cubes in the remaining oil.

3- Add the onions and salt pork to the skillet. Cook one minute over medium heat, stirring constantly with a wooden spoon. Pour the reserved marinad, bring to a boil and cook one minute scraping the bottom of the skillet with a wooden spatula or a spoon. Pour content of the skillet over the beef. Cover and cook 1 1/2 hour until the beef is tender.

4- After one hour, check if the beef is tender and if there is enough liquid; Add cold water if necessary to cover the beef.

GARNISHES

1- Wrap the potatoes individually in aluminum foil and place in the oven one hour before the end of cooking of the casserole. Turn the potatoes over once. 30 minutes before the end, butter four sheets of foil. Wrap 4 carrots in each one. Put in the oven with the potatoes and the casserole.

2- To check the beef, taste a cube. Vegetables are ready when a fork is easily inserted in a potato or carrot. A green salad makes a good accompaniment to this dish.

4 servings

COOKING ON THE BARBECUE

Set the barbecue rack at the highest setting and preheat the barbecue until the temperature reaches about 375°F (190°C), usually the lowest setting on a gas barbecue. Place the meat in a disposable aluminum square pan or an old metal casserole and cover with aluminum foil. Seal well and cook as directed in the conventional method. For garnishes, wrap as indicated in the conventional method and place the potatoes on the second level rack about 45 minutes before the end of cooking of the beef. 20 minutes before the end of cooking of the casserole, add the carrots parcels to the barbecue.

Maple beer ham

The popularity of serving ham at sugarhouses and on the Easter menu takes its origins from traditional preserving techniques. To extend the preservation of some pieces of pork that were frozen in the autumn and stored in the barn for the winter, early settlers smoked the remaining pieces of pork in the spring when the weather became clement.

1	4 to 5 lb (2 kg) ham	1
4 cups	water	1 litre
1	small beer bottle (341 ml)	1
	A few whole cloves	
1/3 cup	maple syrup	80 ml
	Granulated maple sugar (to cover the ham toward the end of the cooking)	

1- Preheat the oven to 325°F (160°C). Rinse the ham in cold water and place in a large saucepan or casserole.

2- Add the water, beer, cloves and maple syrup. Cover and bake 1 1/2 hour or until a long fork comes off easily when inserted in the centre of the ham.

3- Remove the ham form the saucepan and place on a roasting pan. Cover with a thin layer of maple sugar and bake uncovered for another 30 minutes. Let rest for a few minutes before serving.

8 to 12 servings

Oreilles de Christ

It is at the sugarhouse that men began to use the term "oreille de Christ", a disguised swear that women wouldn't allow in the family house. Not without amusement, some men I interviewed admitted that a party at the sugarhouse was an occasion to express themselves in remembrance of the lumber camp life.

Salt pork containing fat only is used to prepare baked beans, pea soup and the crunchy "Oreilles de Christ". Salt pork with some streaks of lean is also used to prepare baked beans as well as beef "bouilli" and grilled slices that are not crunchy.

Salt pork (fat only)

1- Slice the salt pork.

2- Blanch the slices in a saucepan, cover with cold water. Bring to a boil, immediately remove from heat, drain and rinse pork under cold running water.

3- Sauté the slices of salt pork over medium heat in a cast iron skillet. Cook until the slices are crunchy on each side turning them occasionnaly.

Maple pork chops

4	pork chops, 3/4-inch (2 cm) thick	4
1/2 tsp	salt	2 ml
1/4 tsp	ground black pepper	1 ml
2 tbsp	butter	30 ml
2 tbsp	all purpose flour	30 ml
1/4 cup	granulated maple sugar	60 ml
2/3 cup	apple juice	175 ml

1- Preheat the oven to 350°F (175°C).

2- Season the pork chops with salt and pepper.

3- Melt the butter in a large skillet and sauté the pork chops on each side until lightly browned.

4- Place the pork chops in an ovenproof casserole or leave in the skillet. Mix the flour and brown sugar in a small bowl and sprinkle over the chops. Drizzle with apple juice, cover the casserole and bake 40 minutes until tender; it should be easy to tear meat with a fork.

5- Toward the end of the cooking, with the help of a soup spoon, remove excess of fat from the cooking juice.

4 servings

Maple glazed pork roast

This delicious recipe offered by the late doctor Bruce Baker of Stanbridge East in Quebec, was a winner in the Best maple recipes contest of Missisquoi Historical Museum.

There are two kinds of savory on the market; winter savory has a strong and pungent flavour and summer savory has a milder flavour. Most of the Quebec recipes are prepared with winter savory.

1	pork roast of about 3 lb (1 1/2 kg)	1
2	cloves garlic, peeled and cut in half	2
	Salt and pepper	
1 tsp	powdered mustard	5 ml
1	onion, sliced	1
1 tsp	dried savory	5 ml
1 cup	cold water	250 ml
1/4 cup	maple syrup	60 ml

1- Set the oven rack at the lowest position. Preheat the oven to 350°F (180°C). Make 4 incisions in the fat part of the roast and push the pieces of garlic in the incisions. Season the roast with salt and pepper and coat unfatty parts of the roast with dry mustard.

2- Place the onion slices in the middle of a rectangular roasting pan and place the roast on top. Sprinkle savory on the roast and pour 1/3 cup (90 ml) of cold water in the bottom of the dish or just enough to cover the bottom.

3- Bake the roast 2 hours. After the roast has baked 45 minutes, baste every 15 minutes. When the cooking juice begins to brown and dry up, add more water to the dish.

4- Thirty minutes before the end of cooking, remove most of the cooking juice and refrigerate to be able to remove the congealed fat. Drizzle roast with maple syrup and bake another 30 minutes basting twice.

5- Remove the congealed fat that has risen to the top of the cooking juice and add degreased juice to the pan juices. Bake the roast for a few minutes until pan juice is hot.

6 to 8 servings

Pork tenderloin with maple vinegar syrup

Let your taste buds discover a new flavour as you savour these thin slices of pork tenderloin drizzled with maple vinegar syrup. This woody and lightly tart-flavoured syrup will certainly inspire you to use it in other dishes of your own.

8 oz	*pork fillet*	*225 g*
	Salt and pepper	
1 tsp	*vegetable oil*	*5 ml*
1 tsp	*butter*	*5 ml*
1/4 cup	*maple vinegar (preferably from Domaine du PicBois)*	*60 ml*
2 tsp	*vegetable oil*	*10 ml*
1	*small onion, coarsely chopped*	*1*
1 cup	*coarsely chopped mushrooms (cultivated white, oyster or fairy ring mushroom)*	*250 ml*

1- Set the oven rack below center. Preheat the oven to 350°F (180°C).

2- Season the pork with salt and pepper. Heat the oil and butter in a skillet over medium heat and sauté the pork tenderloin until lightly browned on each side.

3- Place the skillet in the oven and bake uncovered for 30 minutes.

4- While the pork tenderloin is baking, pour the maple vinegar in a small saucepan and simmer over low heat until it has a syrupy consistency. Set aside.

5- Take the skillet out of the oven, remove the pork tenderloin and keep warm in the oven.

6- Heat two teaspoons of oil over medium heat in a small skillet and sauté the onions and mushrooms, stirring constantly with a wooden spoon until the vegetables are tendercrisp.

7- To serve, thinly slice the pork tenderloin and overlap on two plates. Garnish with onions and mushrooms. Drizzle maple vinegar syrup over the pork slices.

2 servings

Spareribs

An oriental-flavoured dish that makes a nice addition to a Chinese menu or served with boiled Chinese rice and green vegetables.

1 1/4 lb	spareribs cut into 2-in (5 cm) pieces	625 g
1/4 cup	maple syrup	60 ml
1 tbsp	soy sauce	15 ml
1/4 cup	dry sherry or rice vinegar	60 ml
2	thin slices of fresh ginger	2
1	clove garlic, finely chopped	1
1/4 tsp	salt	1 ml
1/8 tsp	Cayenne pepper	0,5 ml

1- Preheat the oven to 325°F (160°C).

2- Place the ribs in a large pot and cover with cold water. Bring to a boil and drain immediately. Rinse the ribs under cold water and drain again.

3- Lay the ribs in an ovenproof casserole slightly larger than ribs volume.

4- Add the remaining ingredients and bake 2 hours turning the ribs every 30 minutes and brushing with glaze.

2 servings

Photographs:

Spinach and Bean Sprouts Salad (p. 46) ⇒
Maple chicken with vegetables (p. 52) ⇓
Pork tenderloin with maple vinegar syrup (p. 62) ⇓
Maple scalop kebabs (p. 68) with maple-flavoured mussels (p. 67) ⇓

Fish and seafood

Maple grilled salmon steaks

These salmon steaks can be cooked on a barbecue, under the oven broiler or in a grill pan. To preserve the delicate flavour of maple, the salmon steaks are grilled at medium heat and basted with the remaining marinade 2 minutes before the end of cooking.

1/4 cup	maple syrup, preferably medium	60 ml
1 tbsp	cider vinegar	15 ml
1/2 tsp	salt	2 ml
1 1/2 lb	salmon steaks (about 3)	750 g
1/2 tsp	coarsely ground black pepper	2 ml

1- To prepare the marinade: mix maple syrup, vinegar and salt. Place the salmon steaks in a casserole just large enough to fit the steaks and pour the marinade over the steaks. Marinate in the refrigerator for 30 to 60 minutes.

2- Preheat the barbecue, oven broiler or grill pan, remove the salmon from the marinade and let drip to remove the excess marinade. In a small saucepan, bring the marinade to a boil, cook for one minute over high heat.

3- Season the steaks with ground black pepper, grill them 10 minutes per inch (2.5 cm) of thickness, turning the steaks over once while cooking. Two minutes before the end of cooking, generously baste the fish with the remaining marinade. The steaks are done when the flesh is opaque and the bones comes off easily.

2 to 3 servings

Maple-flavoured mussels

If you are a savory aficionado, I suggest you double the quantity required in this recipe. White rice and a green vegetable such as sautéed slices of zucchini or steamed green beans make a nice accompaniment to this dish.

36	mussels	36
3 tbsp	maple syrup	45 ml
7 tbsp	cold water	105 ml
2/3 cup	dry white wine	175 ml
1/2 tsp	dried thyme	2 ml
1/4 tsp	dried savory	1 ml
2 tsp	fresh chopped parsley	10 ml
1	green onion, chopped	1

1- Clean the mussels under cold running water and remove beard as needed. Discard all the mussels that remains open after cleaning. Store in the refrigerator while proceeding with other steps.

2- Pour the maple syrup, cold water and white wine in a large pot. Add the thyme, savory, parsley and green onion, bring to a boil, reduce heat, and simmer uncovered over medium heat for 2 minutes.

3- Add the mussels to the pot, cover and simmer 5 to 10 minutes, stirring once or twice. The mussels are cooked when the shells are opened. Unopenened mussels should be discarded.

4- Serve the mussels in deep bowls drizzled with cooking broth.

2 servings

Maple scallop kebabs

These scallop kebabs can also be served as hors d'oeuvres. To do so, tie the scallops and bacon individually with tooth-picks. Depending on the size of the scallops you will need 4 to 8 scallops per serving for a main dish. Sometimes a fourth of a slice of bacon is sufficient for medium-sized scallops.

Fresh large scallops
Bacon slices, cut in two and half cooked
Maple syrup

1- Surround the scallops with a strip of bacon and thread on a skewer.

2- Preheat the oven broiler or gas barbecue for a few minutes. Baste the kebabs with maple syrup.

3- Grill on one side until lightly browned, turn, baste again, and grill until lightly browned.

Cakes, poudings and pies

Maple cake with a maple meringue icing

CAKE BATTER

2 tbsp	butter	30 ml
3/4 cup	granulated maple sugar	175 ml
2	eggs	2
1/2 tsp	pure vanilla extract	2 ml
1 1/2 cups	all purpose flour	375 ml
1 tbsp	baking powder	15 ml
3/4 cup	milk	175 ml

ICING

2	egg whites	2
	A pinch of salt	
1/3 cup	granulated maple sugar	80 ml
1/4 tsp	baking soda	1 ml

CAKE BATTER

1- Set the oven rack in the center. Preheat the oven to 375°F (190°C). Grease a 8 or 9-inch (23 cm) square pan.

2- Beat the butter and maple sugar until smooth. Beat in one egg at a time scraping the mixing bowl occasionnaly. Mix in vanilla extract.

3- Combine the flour and baking powder in another bowl, add to the first preparation alternating with milk. Beat until smooth.

4- Pour the batter in the pan, bake 30 to 45 minutes until a tooth-pick inserted in the cake comes out clean.

ICING

1- Toward the end of the baking time, pour the egg whites in a glass or stainless steel bowl, free of grease. add salt and whip or beat with an electric beater until soft peak forms. Gradually add the maple sugar and baking soda while beating until the mixture holds its shape when the beaters are lifted. Spread this mixture over the cake and bake another 5 minutes.

9 servings

Maple syrup cheesecake

If you are a cheesecake person, this cake will definitely become one of your favourites. It is the type of dessert I like to prepare for family gatherings, as it is possible to bake the cake 2 to 3 days ahead of time and glaze it just before serving.

BASE

1 1/4 cups	crushed Graham crackers	310 ml
1/4 cup	white sugar	60 ml
1/3 cup	melted butter	75 ml

CHEESE MIXTURE

2	8 oz packs (250 g) of cream cheese, at room temperature	2
2 tbsp	sugar	30 ml
1 tbsp	all purpose flour	15 ml
2	eggs	2
2/3 cup	maple syrup, preferably medium	150 ml
1/2 cup	sour cream	125 ml

ICING

1/2 cup	maple jelly	125 ml

BASE

1- Set the oven rack in the center. Preheat the oven to 350°F (180°C).

2- Combine crumbs, sugar and melted butter in a small mixing bowl or a food processor.

3- Cover the bottom of a 9-inch (23 cm) springform cake pan with the base mixture and press lightly with the palm of the hand. Bake 10 minutes and cool while proceeding with the cake preparation.

4- Reduce the oven temperature to 325°F (160°C).

CHEESE MIXTURE

1- Beat the cream cheese until softened. Beat in the sugar and flour until smooth. Add eggs one at a time. Add the maple syrup, mix well and finish by adding the sour cream. Beat just until smooth.

2- Pour the batter in the cake pan and bake 50 to 60 minutes or until the blade of a butter knife inserted in the center of the cake comes out almost clean. Cool to room temperature.

ICING

1- Heat the maple jelly until liquefied to a spreading consistency. Glaze the cake with a thin layer of the melted jelly. Refrigerate the cheesecake 2 hours before serving.

8 to 10 servings

Apple maple cake pudding

When it is time to pick apples, this dessert will surely become one of your favourites. The tartness of the apple pairs well with the flavour of maple. This pudding is best served at room temperature, drizzled with fresh pouring cream.

APPLE MIXTURE

5	medium apples, peeled and thinly sliced	5
3/4 cup	maple syrup	175 ml

DOUGH

2 tbsp	butter	30 ml
1/4 cup	sugar	60 ml
2	eggs	2
1 cup	all purpose flour	250 ml
1 tsp	baking powder	5 ml
1/2 tsp	salt	2 ml
3 tbsp	milk	45 ml
	Cream	

APPLE MIXTURE

1- Set the oven rack below center. Preheat the oven to 350°F (180°C).

2- Place the apple slices in a deep 9-inch (23 cm) baking pan, drizzle with the syrup. Bake 10 minutes.

BATTER

1- Cream the butter and gradually add sugar. Beat 2 minutes.

2- Add the eggs, beat 2 minutes or until the mixture turns pale.

3- Mix the flour, baking powder and salt, add to the first mixture alternating with the milk. Stop beating as soon as the dry ingredients are incorporated.

4- Drop the batter by spoonfuls on the apples, bake about 20 minutes or until a tooth-pick inserted in the center of the cake comes out clean.

5- Serve warm with or without cream.

6 servings

Maple syrup pudding

This pudding is the cousin of the popular poor man pudding of Quebec. Substituting maple syrup for brown sugar and adding nuts makes it become a luxury treat.

2 tbsp	butter	30 ml
1/4 cup	sugar	60 ml
1	egg	1
1/2 tsp	pure vanilla extract	2 ml
1 cup	all purpose flour	250 ml
2 tsp	baking powder	10 ml
1/4 tsp	salt	1 ml
2/3 cup	milk	150 ml
1/4 cup	chopped nuts	60 ml
1 cup	maple syrup	250 ml

1- Set the oven rack below center. Preheat the oven to 350°F (180°C). Butter the inside of a loaf pan.

2- In a medium mixing bowl, cream the butter and sugar until well blended. Beat in the egg and vanilla extract until mixture whitens.

3- In a second bowl, mix the flour, baking powder and salt. Add to the first mixture, alternating with milk. Beat until smooth, not more.

4- Pour the batter in the buttered pan, sprinkle with nuts and drizzle with maple syrup.

5- Bake 45 minutes until a tooth-pick comes out clean when inserted in the center of the pudding. Serve warm with or without cream.

6 servings

Apple maple crumble

My favourite varieties of apples for pastry making are the tart McIntosh or Granny Smith.

4 cups	peeled and sliced apples	1 litre
2/3 cup	granulated maple sugar	150 ml
1/2 cup	all purpose flour	125 ml
1/2 cup	oatmeal	125 ml
1/3 cup	butter	75 ml

1- Set the oven rack below center. Preheat the oven to 375°F (190°C). Grease an 8-inch (23 cm) square pan.

2- Spread the apple slices in the pan.

3- Mix the maple sugar, flour and oatmeal in a medium mixing bowl. Mix in butter with the help of a pastry blender until light and crumbly. This step can be done in a food processor.

4- Cover the apples with oatmeal flour mixture and bake 30 minutes. Serve warm.

6 to 8 servings

Dumplings in maple syrup

This traditional Quebec dessert is named Grands-Pères in French and means "grandfathers". This comforting dessert is a favourite of Québécois. Resist opening the casserole while the dumplings are cooking and you will get light and smooth dumplings!

DUMPLINGS

1 1/2 cups	all purpose flour	375 ml
1 tbsp	baking powder	15 ml
1/2 tsp	salt	2 ml
3 tbsp	cold butter	45 ml
1/2 cup	milk	125 ml

SAUCE

1 1/4 cups	maple syrup, preferably medium	310 ml
1 cup	cold water	250 ml
1 cup	cream if desired	250 ml

DOUGH

1- Mix the flour, baking powder and salt in a medium mixing bowl. Cut the butter in small pieces and scatter over dry ingredients. Rub the flour mixture and butter between your fingers until the mixture ressemble coarse meal.

2- Add milk and stir until the mixture forms a dough. To mix in a food processor, pulse the dry ingredients a few seconds, scatter the butter around the knife. Pulse a few times until you get the desired texture. Add the milk while the motor is running and stop as soon as a ball forms.

SAUCE

1- Pour the syrup and water in a deep saucepan. Bring to a boil stirring constantly. Drop large spoonfuls of dough in the boiling syrup, spacing each. Reduce heat, cover and simmer 15 minutes. Dumplings are ready when a tooth-pick comes out clean when inserted in dumplings.

2- Cool to lukewarm and serve in deep bowls drizzled with sauce. Top with cream if desired.

6 servings

Rhubarb cobbler

Mrs Winifred Rhodes Beausoleil from Richmond, in the Eastern Townships region of Quebec, has learned how to prepare this cobbler with her late mother. It is made with biscuit dough that blends very well with the contrasting tart flavour of rhubarb and the sweetness of maple syrup.

RHUBARB MIXTURE

3 cups	rhubarb, sliced 1/2-inch (1.5 cm) thick	750 ml
3/4 cup	maple syrup	175 ml
1 tbsp	butter	15 ml

BISCUITS

1 cup	all purpose flour	250 ml
1/4 tsp	salt	1 ml
1/2 tsp	sugar	2 ml
1 1/2 tsp	baking powder	8 ml
1 1/2 tbsp	vegetable shortening	22 ml
1 1/2 tbsp	butter	22 ml
1/3 cup	milk	75 ml
	Melted butter	

RHUBARB MIXTURE

1- Set the oven rack below center. Preheat the oven to 425°F (220°C). Spread the rhubarb in a deep 2-quart (2 litre) casserole, add maple syrup, scatter with the butter.

2- Make the biscuits and cover the rhubarb mixture. Brush the biscuits with melted butter.

3- Bake 20 to 30 minutes until the biscuits are golden. Serve lukewarm with or without pouring cream.

BISCUITS

1- Mix the flour, salt, sugar and baking powder in a medium mixing bowl or in the bowl of a food processor. Add the vegetable shortening and butter, and blend with a pastry blender or pulse until the mixture ressemble coarse meal.

2- Mix in the milk with a fork or a food processor; pulse until the mixture is blended. Place the dough on a floured surface and knead a few times to form a ball.

3- Roll the dough to a thickness of 1/3 inch (1 cm) on a floured surface and cut in about 2-inch (5 cm) rounds.

6 to 8 servings

Maple syrup pie

Mrs Marthe Lacombe, from La Tuque in the Mauricie region, is a talented cook who believes it is important to pass on traditional favourite family recipes. This recipe, which she kindly shared with me, is easy to prepare and has an interesting smooth texture.

1	*unbaked 9-inch (23 cm) pie shell*	1
1	*egg*	1
1 tbsp	*all purpose flour*	15 ml
1 tbsp	*light cream*	15 ml
1 cup	*maple syrup, preferably medium*	250 ml

1- Set the oven rack at the lowest position. Preheat the oven to 400°F (200°C).

2- Beat the egg in a medium mixing bowl, gradually whisk in the flour.

3- Add the cream and maple syrup to the egg mixture and stir until blended, no more.

4- Pour the mixture in the pie shell, bake 25 minutes until firm. Cool to lukewarm before serving.

6 servings

Maple pepper pie

This pie is the favourite dessert of Mrs Sandra Fortier from Stanbridge-East in the Eastern Townships. I must confess I was very much intrigued by the idea of pairing maple with pepper but as soon as I tasted the result, I understood why this dessert is a winner in this part of Quebec. A big thanks to Mrs Fortier for her delicious recipe.

1	unbaked 9-inch (23 cm) pie shell	1
1 cup	granulated maple sugar	250 ml
1 tbsp	all purpose flour	15 ml
1	large egg	1
1 tbsp	melted butter	15 ml
1 cup	heavy cream	250 ml
1/4 tsp	ground black pepper	1 ml

1- Set the oven rack at the lowest position. Preheat the oven to 350°F (180°C).

2- Mix the maple sugar and flour in a small mixing bowl. Beat the egg in a medium mixing bowl. Add maple sugar and flour to the beaten egg. Add the butter, cream and black pepper, stir until well blended.

3- Pour the preparation in the pie shell and bake 30 minutes until firm. Cool to lukewarm before serving.

6 servings

Suet pie

Many remember the taste of this typical dessert. I have learned how to prepare this pie with the late Mrs Gilberte Martinson of La Tuque in the Mauricie region. Suet is often found in the freezer of your supermarket.

1	unbaked 9-inch (23 cm) pie shell	1
2 tbsp	finely chopped beef suet	30 ml
1 cup	shredded maple sugar, from loaf	250 ml
2 tbsp	raisins, cut in half	30 ml

1- Set the oven rack at the lowest position. Preheat the oven to 375°F (190°C).

2- Scatter suet on the bottom of the pie shell, cover with the maple sugar. Garnish with raisins and bake 25 minutes.

3- This pie should be served warm as this brings out the flavour.

6 servings

Maple sugar rolls

A pastry that will satisfy anyone who is found of maple desserts. It has been possible to reproduce this recipe with the help of Mrs Pamela Realfe of Standbridge East, in the Eastern Townships. Some families prepare this pie without the pie shell.

One pie dough recipe (see index)
Butter at room temperature
Granulated or grated maple sugar
Maple syrup
Light cream

1- Set the oven rack below center. Preheat the oven to 400°F (220°C).

2- Roll half of the dough 1/8 inch (1/4 cm) thick, line a 8 or 9-inch (20 or 23 cm) square cake pan.

3- Roll the remaining of pie dough to form a 8 x 18-inch (20 x 46 cm) rectangle. Butter the dough and sprinkle with maple sugar. Beginning with a long end, roll the dough up like a jelly roll. Cut 16 pinwheels, place them spiral side down in the pan, forming four rows.

4- Pour enough maple syrup over the pinwheels to reach a level of 1 1/4 inches (3 cm) . Pour enough cream to fill in pinwheels by 2/3.

5- Bake 20 minutes. Reduce oven temperature to 375°F (190°C) and bake another 20 to 25 minutes or longer until is golden.

8 servings

Apple dumplings, maple sauce

This recipe, first published in my cookbook on the Charlevoix region, was offered to me by Mrs Marcelle Paré from La Malbaie. A talented cook, she has worked many years in the kitchen of a religious community established in the region.

	Pie dough (see index)	
4	apples, peeled and cored	4
	Eggwash (a beaten egg with a bit of milk)	

SAUCE

1 cup	maple syrup	250 ml
1/2 tsp	corn starch	2 ml
1/4 cup	water	60 ml

1- Set the oven rack in the center. Preheat the oven to 375°F (190°C).

2- Roll the dough into four 6-inch (15 cm) squares. Place one apple on each square, moisten the edges of the dough with the eggwash. Bring the corners of the dough on top of the apple, and seal, pinching dough with your fingertips.

3- Place the dumplings on an ungreased cookie sheet and bake 30 to 45 minutes until the dough is golden.

4- Cool to room temperature, drizzle the sauce over the dumpling and serve.

SAUCE

1- Pour the syrup in a small saucepan. Mix the cornstarch and water in a small bowl, add the syrup. Bring to a boil,and simmer for one to two minutes. Pour over dumplings just before serving.

4 servings

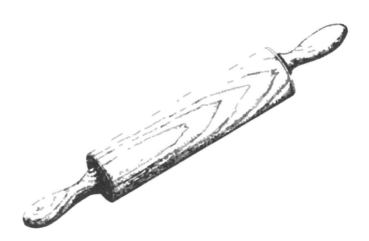

Cookies, bread and muffins

Maple jelly cookies

These cookies are delicious and pretty. I sometimes freeze the dough for later use and bake them at the last minute for unexpected guests.

1/2 cup	butter	125 ml
1/4 cup	granulated maple sugar	60 ml
1	egg yolk	1
1 cup	all purpose flour	250 ml
1/4 tsp	salt	1 ml
1/3 cup	walnuts, finely chopped	75 ml
1/3 cup	maple or apple jelly	75 ml

1- Set the oven rack in the center. Preheat the oven to 350°F (180°C).

2- Beat the butter and maple sugar in a medium-sized bowl.

3- Add the egg yolk and beat until well blended.

4- Mix the flour and salt, and gradually mix in the first mixture. If the dough is too soft, refrigerate 30 minutes before shaping the cookies.

5- Shape the dough in 1-inch (2,5 cm) balls, rolling dough between the palm of your hands, roll in chopped nuts and place on an ungreased cookie sheet well apart. Press down the center of each cookie with your thumb and fill with a little maple jelly. Bake one sheet at a time 15 minutes.

6- Cool for one minute, remove cookies with a spatula and place on a cake rack to cool. Store in an airtight box.

About 20 cookies

Maple cookies

These cookies can be eaten plain or spread with maple butter.

1	egg	1
1 tbsp	melted butter at room temperature	15 ml
1/2 cup	maple syrup at room temperature	125 ml
1 cup	flour	250 ml
1 1/4 tsp	baking powder	6 ml
	A pinch of salt	
1/2 cup	finely chopped pecans	125 ml
	Whole pecans	

1- Set the oven rack in the center. Preheat the oven to 325°F (160°C).

2- Beat the egg in a small bowl, mix in the butter and maple syrup.

3- Mix the flour, baking powder and salt in a second bowl and stir in the first mixture until well blended. Blend in the pecan nuts.

4- Using two teaspoons, drop 1 1/2-inch (4 cm) balls of dough on an ungreased cookie sheet, leaving a 2-inch (5 cm) space between cookies. Press a whole pecan on each cookie.

5- Bake one sheet at a time for 10 minutes. Cool for one minute, remove from the cookie sheet and cool on a cake rack. Store in an airtight jar.

20 cookies

Maple pecan squares

I am indebted to Mrs Florence Dupuis as she shared one of her favourite maple recipes. These marvellous squares can be offered as a gift or brought to a picnic.

BASE

1 cup	all purpose flour	250 ml
1/4 cup	brown sugar	60 ml
1/2 cup	butter	125 ml

FILLING

1 cup	maple syrup	250 ml
1/2 cup	brown sugar	125 ml
2	large eggs	2
1/4 cup	butter at room temperarure	60 ml
1/4 tsp	salt	1 ml
2 tbsp	all purpose flour	30 ml
1/2 tsp	pure vanilla extract	2 ml
2/3 cup	coarsely chopped pecans	150 ml

BASE

1- Set the oven rack below center. Preheat the oven to 300°F (150°C).

2- Mix the flour and brown sugar in a medium-sized bowl. Cut in the butter with a pastry blender and work until the mixture begins to hold its shape. Finish binding the mixture with your fingertips. This step can be done in a food processor: pulse the flour and brown sugar.Add the butter around the knife and pulse until a ball forms. Scrape the bowl once or twice while mixing.

3- Press the dough in a greased 9-inch (23 cm) square cake pan with the palm of your hands. Bake 10 minutes and cool to lukewarm.

FILLING

1- Mix the maple syrup and brown sugar in a medium saucepan. Bring to a boil stirring constantly with a wooden spoon. Reduce the heat and simmer over low heat for 5 minutes. Cool.

2- Increase the oven temperature to 450°F (230°C). Beat the eggs and pour in the cooled maple syrup mixture in a thin stream, stirring constantly. Beat in the butter, salt, flour and vanilla extract until well blended. Add the pecans and pour over the precooked base. Bake 10 minutes, reduce the oven temperature to 350°F (180°C) and bake for another 20 minutes. Cool completely and cut into squares.

16 squares

Maple nut muffins

This recipe is an adaptation of a recipe found in old cookbooks published on Quebec cuisine. The flavour of these muffins is at its best when they are freshly baked. I suggest you freeze them if you wish to serve them on future occasion.

TOPPING

1/3 cup	melted butter	75 ml
1/3 cup	chopped nuts	75 ml
1/2 cup	maple syrup	125 ml

MUFFINS BATTER

2 cups	all purpose flour	500 ml
2 tsp	baking powder	10 ml
1/4 tsp	baking soda	1 ml
1 tsp	salt	5 ml
1	egg	1
3 tbsp	maple syrup	45 ml
1 cup	milk	250 ml
1/4 cup	melted butter at room temperature	60 ml

1- Set the oven rack in the center. Preheat the oven to 400°F (200°C).

TOPPING

1- Grease 12 muffin tins, pour one teaspoon (5 ml) of melted butter in each muffin tin. Divide the nuts and the 1/2 cup (125 ml) of maple syrup among the 12 muffin tins.

MUFFINS BATTER

1- Mix the flour, baking powder, baking soda and salt in a large mixing bowl. In another bowl, beat the egg, add the maple syrup, milk and melted butter.

2- Pour the liquid mixture over the first mixture and stir to blend.

3- Fill muffins tins to about two-thirds full with a large spoon. Bake 15 to 20 minutes until a tooth-pick inserted in the center of a muffin comes out clean.

4- Turn the muffins upside down, let drip a few seconds and remove muffin tins.

12 muffins

Maple nut bread

This bread is good plain but, if you spread it with maple sugar butter, it is delectable! You can freeze the bread and prepare the maple sugar butter just before serving.

2	eggs	2
3 tbsp	vegetable oil	45 ml
1/2 cup	milk	125 ml
1 cup	maple syrup, preferably medium	250 ml
2 1/2 cups	all purpose flour	625 ml
1 tbsp	baking powder	15 ml
1/8 tsp	baking soda	0.5 ml
1/2 tsp	salt	2 ml
1 cup	chopped walnuts	250 ml

BUTTER

1/2 cup	unsalted or half salt butter, at room temperature	125 ml
1/3 cup	granulated maple sugar	80 ml

1- Set the oven rack in the center. Preheat the oven to 375°F (190°C). Grease a 9 x 5 x 3-inch (23 x 13 x 6 cm) loaf pan.

2- Beat the eggs in a large bowl until well blended. Add the oil, milk and maple syrup and mix. (...continued p.97)

Crisp crêpes (p. 34) ⇒

3- In another mixing bowl, combine the flour, baking powder, baking soda and salt. Gradually add the egg mixture and stir until just blended. Add the walnuts and pour the dough in the prepared pan. Bake 45 to 60 minutes until a tooth-pick inserted in the center of the loaf comes out clean. Cool 5 minutes, turn out on a cake rack and cool.

BUTTER

1- Mix the butter and maple sugar and spread on the slices of maple nut loaf as desired.

One loaf, 16 servings

Cold desserts

Slice of bread with cream and maple sugar

This is the simplest dessert to prepare and one of the favourite desserts of Québécois. Some like to sprinkle the sugar on the slice of bread and then pour the cream while others prefer pouring the cream first and cover it with sugar.

One slice of white country bread

Best quality heavy cream

Freshly grated maple sugar from sugarloaf

1- Place a slice of bread on a plate, cover with cream and sprinkle with plenty of maple sugar.

1 serving

Maple syrup rice pudding

	Cold water	
1/2 tsp	salt	2 ml
1/3 cup	rice, non converted	75 ml
3 tbsp	corn starch	45 ml
1/2 cup	maple syrup	125 ml
1 1/2 cups	milk	375 ml
2	egg yolks	2
	Maple syrup for serving	

1- Fill a medium saucepan to two-thirds full with cold water. Add salt and bring to a boil. Add the rice and boil 20 to 30 minutes until tender. Drain well.

2- Place the cornstarch in a small bowl and gradually whisk in the maple syrup.

3- In a medium saucepan heat the milk over low heat; milk should not boil. Add the maple syrup mixture to warm milk and bring to a boil over medium heat, stirring constantly with a wooden spoon. Simmer until the sauce thickens. Remove from heat.

4- Beat the egg yolks, warm slowly with a few spoonfuls of hot maple sauce, stirring constantly with a wooden spoon. Gradually pour the mixture in a thin stream in the maple sauce stirring constantly. Simmer the sauce for 2 minutes.

5- Mix the cooked rice and sauce, pour in small bowls. Store in the refrigerator. At serving time, pour one tablespoon of maple syrup on each pudding.

6 servings

Maple custards, strawberry coulis

CUSTARD

3	large eggs	3
1 cup	lukewarm milk	250 ml
1/2 cup	light cream	125 ml
2/3 cup	maple syrup	175 ml
1/4 tsp	salt	1 ml
3 tbsp	maple liqueur if desired	45 ml

STRAWBERRY COULIS

3 cups	fresh strawberries	750 ml
	Sugar	

CUSTARD

1- Preheat the oven to 350°F (180°C).

2- Beat the eggs in a medium-sized bowl until foamy.

3- In another bowl, combine the milk, cream, maple syrup and salt, and gradually stir in the egg mixture.

4- Pour the custard in about 4-ounce (125 ml) lightly oiled ramekins. Place the ramekins in a big rectangular baking pan and pour about one inch of lukewarm water in the pan. Bake 30 minutes until the blade of a knike comes out almost clean when inserted in the custard. Cool to room temperature and refrigerate for 6 to 8 hours.

5- Unmold each custard on a dessert plate and pour enough coulis around the custard to cover the bottom of the plate. Garnish with a fresh strawberry if desired.

STRAWBERRY COULIS

1- Puree the strawberries in a blender or a food processor. Add a few spoonfuls of sugar and process to blend.

8 servings

Maple mousse

This mousse is easy to prepare and has a light and silky texture. A dessert that can be served as is or garnished with fresh strawberries, raspberries, blueberries or Mandarin oranges.

1 tbsp	cold water	15 ml
1 1/2 tsp	gelatin	7 ml
1/2 cup	maple syrup	125 ml
1 cup	heavy cream	250 ml

1- Pour the cold water in a small mixing bowl, sprinkle the gelatin over the water and let stand for a few minutes until translucent.

2- Pour the maple syrup in a small saucepan and heat up until hot but do not let it boil. Remove the saucepan from the heat and stir in the gelatin mixture until melted. Cool to lukewarm before proceeding with the remaining steps.

3- Pour the cream in a large mixing bowl and whip until it holds its shape on the beaters.

4- At low speed, mix maple gelatin mixture in cream. Pour the mousse in four to six dessert cups and refrigerate for at least 2 hours before serving.

4 to 6 servings

Apple maple mousse

This refreshing apple mousse is an adaptation of the recipe of my late mother-in-law Rebbeca Dontigny. It was one of her favourite recipes when apples where picked. To prevent the apples from darkening, they should be peeled and grated just before they are added to the whipped egg whites. It is preferable not to prepare this dessert more than one hour before serving.

2	egg whites	2
	A pinch of salt	
3 tbsp	granulated maple sugar	45 ml
3/4 cup	peeled grated tart apple (Granny, Smith or McIntosh) about 3 medium apples	175 ml

1- Place the egg whites in an medium-sized enamel or stainless steel mixing bowl. Add a pinch of salt and beat the egg whites until soft peaks forms.

2- Gradually mix in maple sugar and beat until firm peaks forms.

3- Fold in the grated apple and spoon in 4 desserts cups. Refrigerate until ready to serve.

4 servings

Fresh fruits in maple cream sauce

Mrs Madeleine Lafond of Trois-Rivières says this is one of the favourite desserts of her family. Any kind of fruit can be added to the sauce.

1 tbsp	butter	15 ml
2 tbsp	all purpose flour	30 ml
1 cup	heavy cream	250 ml
1 cup	maple syrup	250 ml
	Fresh fruits like strawberries, raspberries, bananas, apples, kiwis, etc...	

1- Melt the butter in a medium saucepan and whisk in the flour.

2- Gradually mix the cream and maple syrup into the butter and flour mixture. Bring to a boil over medium heat, stirring constantly with a wooden spoon. Reduce heat and simmer until the sauce thickens.

3- Cool completely, add fruits and stir gently to coat with sauce. Serve in dessert cups.

6 to 8 servings

> **KITCHEN TIP**
>
> Cream whips faster if very cold. When the weather is hot, place the mixing bowl and beaters in the freezer for a few minutes before whipping. Watch well while beating; overwhipped cream easily turns into butter.

Maple syrup flavoured oranges

2   *large navel oranges*
1/4 cup   *maple syrup*   *60 ml*

1- Remove one piece of orange zest (orange part only) and slice thinly to get 1 teaspoon (5 ml) of julienne strips.

2- Peel the oranges completely to the flesh with a paring knife. Remove the segments between membranes with a paring knife and place in a bowl. Press the remaining membrane juice over the segments.

3- Place the zest in a small saucepan, cover with cold water, bring to a boil and simmer for one minute. Drain the zest, put back in to the saucepan and add the maple syrup. Simmer 2 minutes and pour over the orange segments.

4- Refrigerate for at least one hour before serving.

2 to 4 servings

Maple penuche

Traditionally, the cooking of this candy was measured by dropping a small amount of the mixture in cold water. The cooking of the candy was done when it formed a ball. Experienced cooks can still refer to that method but I think that nowadays it is more accurate to use a candy thermometer to check if the candy is ready to cool. A very handy kitchen tool for any amateur cook.

The best nuts to add to penuche are hazelnuts, walnuts and pecan nuts. Shelled walnuts are best kept in the freezer; no need to defrost before adding them to the dishes.

1 1/2 cup	maple syrup	375 ml
1/2 cup	white sugar	125 ml
1 cup	heavy cream	250 ml
1 cup	chopped nuts, if desired	250 ml

1- Butter a loaf pan and set aside.

2- Pour the maple syrup in a deep medium-sized saucepan. Add the sugar and mix well. Mix in the cream.

3- Bring the mixture to a boil over medium heat, stirring constantly with a wooden spoon. Simmer without stirring until the candy thermometer reaches 240°F (116°C). Remove the saucepan from heat and let rest until the temperature reaches 104°F (40°C).

4- Beat the mixture vigorously with a wooden spoon until it whitens and begin to hold its shape. Promptly add the nuts and pour the candy in the buttered pan.

5- Let stand for a few minutes and cut in small squares before the mixture has completely cooled. Place squares in an airtight container, placing a sheet of wax paper between the layer of candies.

6- Candies can be stored at room temperature for 5 days, or 3 months in the freezer.

Maple taffy

You would like to treat yourself to maple taffy and all you have in your cupboard is a can of maple syrup; then why not spoil yourself by making your own maple taffy? All you need is a candy thermometer and it will be very easy to do!

1 cup   *maple syrup*   *250 ml*

1- Lightly butter the inside of a deep small saucepan and pour the syrup in the saucepan. Bring to a boil over medium heat, reduce heat and simmer until a candy thermometer reaches 238°F (114°C). Frequently watch the thermometer.

2- Let stand for one minute and pour in a small plastic container. If a foam forms on top of the candy, remove it with a spoon.

3- Close the plastic container and immerse completely in cold water for one hour. Remove from the cold water, uncover and pour 1 teaspoon of cold water on top of the taffy, tilting the container to completely cover the taffy. Store in the refrigerator.

TAFFY ON SNOW

1- Plan the cooking of the candy just before serving time.

2- Before beginning the cooking of the candy, fill large containers with clean packed snow.

3- When ready to serve, pour hot taffy over the snow, forming long ribbons of 1 inch (2,5 cm). Cool one or two minutes and roll on wooden sticks or spoons.

Various

Pie dough

Through the years, I developed my own way to prepare pie dough. By pouring the cold water here and there over the dry ingredients, it takes less time to bind and prevent excessive manipulating, which is the main reason for tough pie dough. Also, when rolling, I suggest turning the piece of dough once or twice while proceeding. This prevents the dough from sticking to the working surface.

The dough can be wrapped in a piece of wax paper, stored in a plastic bag and placed in the refrigerator for 5 days or frozen for 3 months. Bring to room temperature before using. Don't be scared to fail and don't forget not to roll the dough too thin to make sure the crust will have room to flake!

2 2/3 cups	all purpose flour	675 ml
1 tsp	salt	5 ml
1 cup	vegetable shortening	250 ml
1 cup	cold water	250 ml

1- Mix the flour and salt in a large bowl. Cut the vegetable shortening in six pieces, scatter over the flour mixture. Cut the shortening in the flour with a pastry blender until the mixture forms particles the size of a pea.

2- Sprinkle the cold water over the mixture and blend by passing a fork through the mixture until it begins to form a ball. If needed, add more water, a few tablespoons at a time, to bind the dough in a ball. Finish working the dough with your hands but do not over-manipulate, otherwise it will be though.

3- Wrap the dough in wax paper and let stand a few minutes before using. At this point, the dough can be refrigerated for 3 days or frozen cut into three or four pieces but should be brought back to room temperature before using.

4- On a floured board, roll the pieces of dough to a thickness of 1/4 inch (0.5 cm) turning and flipping at least once during this operation; this will prevent the dough from sticking to the board.

DOUBLE CRUST PIE

Seal the crusts with an eggwash (mixture of one egg beaten with a little milk) and brush the top crust with the same mixture, except the pie rim. Slit the top crust a few times before baking.

BAKED PIE SHELL

Prick the shell and place a light pie plate or a few light aluminium pie plates for the first 15 minutes of baking. Remove the pie plate to finish baking; pie plate will easily be removed when it's time to take it off. Cook for another 10 to 15 minutes until the pie shell is light brown.

3 to 4 crusts

Maple barbecue sauce

This sauce is ideal for pork and chicken. The cooking can be done in the oven or on a barbecue. This recipe gives a fairly good quantity that can be divided and frozen in small containers for future use. It can also be refrigerated for 2 weeks.

1	28 oz (796 ml) canned whole tomatoes or 6 red tomatoes in season, peeled	1
1	large onion, finely chopped	1
4	shallots	1
2	cloves garlic, finely chopped	2
1	bay leave	1
1/2 tsp	dried thyme	2 ml
1/3 cup+2 tbsp	maple syrup	110 ml
2 tsp	cider vinegar	10 ml
1/2 tsp	Cayenne pepper	2 ml
1 tbsp	coarse salt	15 ml
1/4 c. thé	pepper	1 ml

1- Core the tomatoes, cut in two and remove seeds.

2- Place all the ingredients in a large stainless steel saucepan. Simmer over low heat for one to two hours until the sauce thickens. Stir the sauce frequently with a wooden spoon.

3- Puree the sauce in a blender or food processor.

4- If the sauce is used to baste a big chicken or a big piece of meat, begin basting when half cooked.

Sap tea

The sugar maker makes tea with maple sap and I thought it would be nice to try that at home. I calculated how much cold water should be combined with maple syrup and I was delighted to discover how delicate the taste of tea is when infused in this homemade sap.

2 1/4 cups	*cold water*	*560 ml*
1 tbsp	*maple syrup*	*15 ml*
2 tsp	*black tea (approximately)*	*10 ml*

1- Pour the cold water in a small saucepan, add the maple syrup and mix a few seconds to dissolve syrup. Bring to a boil.

2- While homemade sap is heating, place black tea in a tea infuser.

3- Pour the boiling homemade sap in a teapot, add infuser and let steep for 5 minutes. Serve.

2 servings

SUGARHOUSE MENU

Oreilles de Christ

Maple beer ham

Maple syrup baked beans

Eggs in syrup

Boiled potatoes

Country bread

Pickled cucumbers

Crisp Crêpes

Taffy on snow

MAPLE DELIGHT

Spinach and goat cheese salad

Maple grilled lamb chops

Oven roasted vegetables

Rice

Maple cake with maple meringue icing

USEFUL ADDRESSES

FÉDÉRATIONS DES PRODUCTEURS ACÉRICOLES DU QUÉBEC

555 Boul. Roland-Therrien

Longueuil, QC J4Y 3Y9

514-679-0530

www.maple-erable.qc.ca/f_sirop.html

INSTITUT QUÉBÉCOIS DE L'ÉRABLE

1290 av. Trudelle,

Plessisville, QC G6L 1T9

800-372-2530

To buy maple products go to www.erable.org

To visit a sugarhouse or plan a meal at the sugarhouse go to www.laroutedessucres.com

BIBLIOGRAPHY

Dupont, Jean-Claude, Le sucre du pays, Léméac, Montréal 1975.

Provencher, Jean, Les quatre saisons dans la vallée du Saint-Laurent, Boréal, Montréal 1988.

Lessard, Michel, Objets anciens du Québec, La vie domestique, Les Éditions de l'Homme, Montréal 1994

Paul-André Leclerc, La Belle Histoire des sucres, Musée François-Pilote, La Pocatière, 1991

James M. Lawrence et Rux Martin, Sweet Maple, Chapters, Shelburne 1993._

Kalm, Pehr, Voyage de Pehr Kalm en 1749, Éditions Pierre Tisseyre, Montréal, 1977

CONVERSION CHART

1/8 teaspoon	0,5 ml
1/4 teaspoon	1 ml
1/2 teaspoon	2 ml
1 teaspoon	5 ml
1 tablespoon	15 ml
1/4 cup	60 ml
1/3 cup	80 ml
1/2 cup	125 ml
3/4 cup	180 ml
1 cup	250 ml
4 cups	1 l

Oven temperature

200°F	100°C
225	110
250	120
275	140
300	150
325	160
350	180
375	190
400	200
425	220
450	230
475	240
500	260
525	270
550	290

Index

A

B

C

H

HAM

L

LAMB

M

MAPLE PRODUCTS

MOUSSE

MUFFINS

MUSSELS

O

P

T

V